THISTLEDOWN

Poems for UNICEF

Edited by John F Deane

 **DEDALUS**

I am not yet born; O fill me
With strength against those who would freeze my
humanity, would dragoon me into a lethal automaton,
would make me a cog in a machine, a thing with
one face, a thing, and against all those
who would dissipate my entirety, would
blow me like thistledown hither and
thither or hither and thither
like water held in the
hands would spill me.
— Louis MacNeice

"Prayer Before Birth"
(Collected Poems; Faber & Faber)

The Dedalus Press
24 The Heath, Cypress Downs, Dublin 6. Ireland

This is a special publication, published on 6th November 1990, all proceeds from sales of the book and from sales of the original poems and paintings reproduced in the book, will go to UNICEF. The printing of the book is sponsored by Eagle Star, Dublin.

Cover Painting by ROBERT BALLAGH

CONTENTS

Editorial

I am deeply grateful to the poets and artists included in this collection, all of whom responded with generosity to the request for material. The intention of the book is to create awareness of the plight of children throughout the world by presenting works of art that are inspired by the theme of childhood, thus prodding memory and suggesting contrasts; and to raise much-needed funds to support the work of UNICEF.

It would also be a hope that the book would generate sufficient interest to pressurize our government into passing the Childcare Bill, thus clearing the way for Ireland to ratify the Convention on the Rights of the Child which has already been ratified by some 26 countries.

I am grateful to Eagle Star for acting as sponsors in the printing of this book; the gesture is a generous one and deeply encouraging.

John F Deane, August 1990

The quotations in prose are taken from "The State of the World's Children 1990", published for UNICEF by Oxford University Press.

UNICEF

The creative imagination knows no boundaries. It reaches across barriers of race, religion and class, culture and politics in response to human experience. Poets have often written about childhood and no doubt always will, since the formative years are so stimulating and so vulnerable. So much happens in the life of the child that it is inevitable the adult will feel drawn to explore the early years, to repossess what was so fundamental but incompletely understood and often obscured in the passage of time.

In central ways the story of UNICEF corresponds to the activities of the creative imagination. Founded in 1946 to take care of the needs of European children after the war, it has extended across the world to over a hundred countries, responding to the recurrent needs of children and families in different regions, gaining experience and understanding in the process, and bringing an increasing skill, competence and knowledge to bear on the needs of children. UNICEF not only brings aid in the form of food and medicines, it also brings education and awareness. It trains people in the developing world to take better care of mothers and children. Today UNICEF is composed of a vast network of experienced and professional people. It responds to the persistent and changing needs of the people and does so quickly and intelligently, taking advantage of the latest developments in medical science and in communications. It fulfills a basic trust. "Mankind", says the Declaration of the Rights of the Child, "owes the child the best that it has to give." The appeal of the child to our love and protection is inescapable.

The Irish National Committee for UNICEF, established thirty years ago, is part of the UNICEF network, one of thirty-five national committees, most of whom are volunteers, who support professionals in the field. Our main function is to raise funds and provide information. We raise funds particularly through the sale of greeting cards and through our annual Children's Appeal. We are happy to celebrate our thirtieth anniversary through John F Deane's imaginative collection of poems and paintings.

Maurice Harmon
President

Great change is in the air as the 1990s begin. And great change is needed if a century of unprecedented progress is not to end in a decade of decline and despair for half the nations of the world. In many countries poverty, child malnutrition, and ill health are advancing again after decades of steady retreat. And although the reasons are many and complex, overshadowing all is the fact that the governments of the developing world as a whole have now reached the point of devoting *half of their total annual expenditures* to the maintenance of the military and the servicing of debt. These two essentially unproductive activities are now costing the nations of Africa, Asia, and Latin America almost £1 billion every day, or more than £400 a year for each family in the developing world. Half-way through this century, President Eisenhower described the vast scale of military expenditure as "humanity hanging from a cross of iron": if he were alive to observe the impact of the debt crisis as the century comes to an end, then he would have to add that humanity is also hanging from a cross of gold.

SEAN DUNNE

THE JEWISH MUSEUM IN PORTOBELLO

Ireland, they say, has the honour of being the
only country which never persecuted the jews. Do
you know that? And do you know why?...
— Why, sir? Stephen asked, beginning to smile.
— Because she never let them in, Mr Deasy said
solemnly.

Ulysses

Two candles on a kitchen table,
Glazed bread beneath a cloth.
You lean against cool walls
As if to dodge a searchlight.

Edelstein? You're called Edelstein?
Exile hovers around your name —
All that's left of your lost father
Fleeing from Nazis in Dortmund.

Shreds of barbed wire from a camp,
A swastika on a polished badge.
Give me instead old Mushatt the chemist,
His balms and potions to ease a graze.

Our fingers laced like plaited loaves,
We stand before unrolled scrolls.
I see you pleading behind camp gates,
Your hair flung among the hair of thousands.

Your father is a quiet ghost moving
In the sealed ghetto of childhood.
The souvenir mug he gave you survives,
An ark of memory you never forsake.

In Wine's shop in Terenure, I buy
Rye bread, chunks of kosher cheese.
Streetlights are a bright menorah
Lit with singing for our feast.

Your father lacked Abraham's luck,
Abandoned by angels on the Sabbath.
His loss is a closing of synagogues,
The fading of black from prayer-straps.

We kiss under a canopy of clouds,
Closer than a skull-cap to its skull.
Loss is a covenant between us,
The burnt bread of your father's exile.

JOHN ENNIS

HIBISCUS

The old rose-petalled gods tremble yet remain ungraved.
When I planted that butchered stub-trunk of hibiscus
Last March, I didn't know what its blooms envisaged.
Survive these days, like dumb animals, if needs must

Flourishing among your far provincial urns like a memory.
For the eyes of strangers you blur-burn with a message.
From early June on, till the severer frosts of winter
That's long enough: no one other tree has your courage

Up whose slender armlets bloom after bloom comes until
The tip is reached way past equinox and berried Samhain
Long after the righting of our first August-tossed petals
When the very bees have long clustered, their well-laden

Pollen baskets are empty of your open-housed pink dust.
You have grown part of us to limb and flower universally.
Where blossoms are snipped, and minds may not endure,
You stand, too, at that youthful, stamen-crushed extremity.

In Hibiscus Town the people will in their time eat bean
Curd again, make every meal a feast. This November noon,
Sentinel at my foggy gate, it is too far for you to hear
The latest slob out on the make, belting his gong for revolution.

MAMAFESTA FOR SUMMER

Singer of old light operetta
Gleanings from the Ursuline,
Ours is the free prison.
The sheets are flapping in the wind.
There is a shower coming over the wood.
It is down upon us before
The red pegs spatter the blue basin.

Anne, bringer of coffees
And pluralities of buns
Ovened with care and currants,
The young are dragging out of us
We disgorge our craws for them
And they think, this is how it should be.
Their laughter splits our skulls.

Our days have no linear
Motion, they spill over the rims
Of twilight and sunrise and circle
These vacation weeks
Whetting our whelksome appetites.
The nightmare is a phone call away
Outside the copper hedges

Tempered by grisellenia
And hibiscus leaning to the road.
Wild rose tangles
Beebloom, too, then berry into winter.
The grass is wet.
But the sun lords it on the horizon.
Will it be a pet day?

There was a squall at 3 a.m.
This is history at our backs
Though the sea at Dunmore
Is rumbling at the cliffs.
Here, at six o seven
A sizzle of bees
Fills the escallonia.

The pools of light are stirred.
The slates are cracking in the sun.
The clouds are shifting south
And where great banks
Of blackness mounded,
Blue smoothes the sky
Across the Rock.

The Babel of voices begins.
In the kitchen, TV native and antipodean.
The bowls are stacked with cereal.
Spoons are bickering in cups.
Milk blots. Sugar spills.
Through a window I note how the juniper
Outgrows its corner.

Bicycles orbit the gravel
Giddying round the house.
Cut knees. Gritted wounds.
Give us the usual shore forays
Dragging the family with rough strife
Through the dogrose
Petalled gates.

On my own for the tea
I envy the seagod
Slouching out to ocean
His shore-thunder muted.
Hiving bees is easier.
Soon herself will phone
To see all is well, at peace.

Well, they were well
The last time I saw them.
Bedlam carries up the field
To the nectar-misted apiary
Where I add super to super
Presumptive of better weather,
As sisters cuff their brothers
In the last test of the day.

R. S. THOMAS (Wales)

OBJECT

Look at this object.
What is it,
Money is its name.
Money is the Esperanto
that carries it
the world over. The glair
of its passage
is on every sky.
It builds its retreat
of gold, hoping to dazzle
death itself. It wears
gold, but death is within.
Death contaminates
everything it touches.
It is what it brings,
inflationary as its shadow,
to the young children
who would play in the sun.

It is the greatest comdemnation of our times that more than a quarter of a million small children should still be dying *every week* of easily preventable illness and malnutrition. *Every day* measles, whooping cough and tetanus, all of which can be prevented by an inexpensive course of vaccines, kill almost 8,000 children. *Every day* diarrhoeal dehydration, which can be prevented at almost no cost, still kills almost 7,000 children. *Every day* pneumonia, which can be treated by low-cost antibiotics, kills more than 6,000 children. Death and suffering on this scale is simply no longer necessary, and it is therefore no longer acceptable. Morality must march with capacity.

"Door Into the Dark", Lithograph *by* ANNE MADDEN

MICHAEL HAMBURGER (England)

IN LONDON II: FOR CLAIRE

Housing love, that is hard enough,
Both for children and for another making
In disorder give it a base, a place;
Harder still, though, to lavish it homeless,
Shapes and music and words running loose
For the sake of community, healing.

Mainstreet, market affirm a commingling of needs,
And for progress there's traffic along them;
Not the cinema's gutted hulk,
Side street hiding abandoned workshops,
Boarded windows, doorways that frame a darkness,
Best endeavour shamed by the plain clean lines
Of the ancient alms-house grown alien, remote.

On the bus, from his mother's lap
More than once the little black boy reaches out
For the book a stranger is reading,
Grieves when the pages are turned.
She, the reader, is kind, but the book will close.

Less confined than most, the rabbit in your back yard,
Though unmated, leaves you no plant that can flower,
Freely ranging there, still is thwarted,
For subsistence held within bounds of the given,
For fulfilment driven to break those bounds.
So, picked up to be fondled, he clawed
Your small daughter, punishing your love through hers.

As I limp through Hackney, a visitor merely,
Lamed elsewhere, on grounds that look different,
What to you can I say of setbacks, who live
Where the poor are punished for paining the better-off
And unease, become hate, has knotted the law for lashing?
What of love that defies them, my stubborn daughter?
Only that between us which needs no saying:
All's despite, all our making a making-do.

There we meet again, with a home in common.

MICHAEL HAMBURGER

ESCAPE

"Look, a white bird!"
She called out, at her street-side window,
But as it flew from the hawthorn tree
Saw the white merge
In pale yellow, the strangeness dwindle
To a common cagebird's escape.

Perched there, against red berries
And the yellowing leaves,
It had seemed white, an albino finch
Or some rare exotic visitor,
Yet in its right place, free;
Not mobbed by blackbirds or sparrows.

Identifying, she doomed it:
No bird hatched in captivity,
She'd learnt, can survive many days,
Let alone a winter, of freedom.
"A cage, and seed. Quick!"

But the bird had moved on,

Into who knows what harshness
Of hunger, predators, winds;
Out of our range too,
Safe from the lure of the half-life,
Ours, that we might have restored
For the sake of comfort, our own.

13

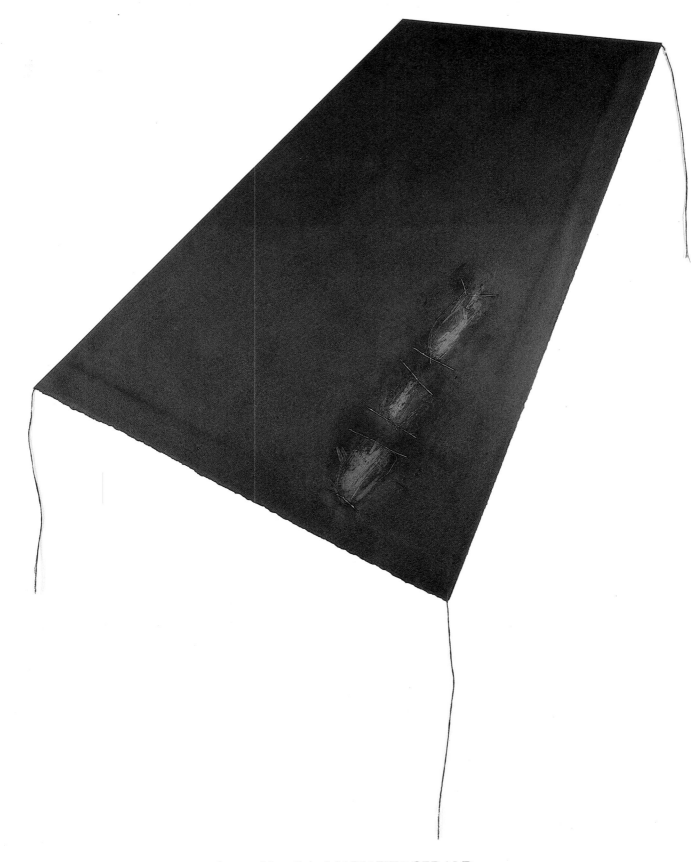

"Counter No. 4", by MARY FITZGERALD

JOSEPH PAUL SCHNEIDER (France)

ALPHABET

Dans les larmes de l'enfant, je retrouve, comme dans un miroir, le petit garçon que je connais bien. J'ai vu passer sur son visage cette même ombre d'une plaie quand, humilié, il s'entêtait à sourire.

Enfance d'eau vive, tes paradis ne sont pas tourjours verts. J'ai fréquenté tes pays de détresse sans horizon, pays de cris noués, de silences sans noms, de nuits gommées par l'insomnie. A rebours du ciel, le ciel s'obscurcit dans les forêts closes où se réfugie l'enfant blessé. Les larmes épuisent parfois plus qu'elles ne libèrent.

Petit garçon: ramasse ce caillou. Tiens-le serré dans le nid de ta main.

Poing qui saigne, tu avances dans la lumière tranchante vers le grand tableau du parti pris de vivre où le jour crayeux t'apprend l'alphabet de la solitude.

JOSEPH PAUL SCHNEIDER (France)

ALPHABET

In the tears of the child, I recognise, as in a mirror, the small boy I know well. I have seen that same shadow of a hurt pass across his face when, though humiliated, he kept smiling obstinately.

Childhood of spring water, your Edens are not always green. I have travelled your lands of boundless distress, lands of choked-back cries, of nameless silences, of nights jammed by sleeplessness. Opposed to the sky, the sky darkens in the dense forests where the hurt child takes refuge. Tears exhaust, at times, much more than they relieve.

Little boy: pick up this stone. Grip it tightly in the nest of your hand.

Bleeding fist, you come forward in the cutting light towards the great blackboard of commitment to living where chalky daylight teaches you the alphabet of solitude.
(translated from the French, by J.F.Deane)

PAUL MURRAY

NIGHT THOUGHT

Between the stars
there will be no peace
between the islands
no rest

until the eyes
of the smallest creatures
reach
to the far-off Pleiades;

and the shadow
that falls
between moment and moment
is lost in the sun.

PAUL MURRAY

THRESHOLD

Not at the pointed
hour of ecstasy
nor at the furthest edge
of being,
but here, in the even
close-knit hours,
among the weekday
goings-on
of wind and weather,
here is our hidden threshold
of perception,
here we must wait
until the door of the present
swings open
on its new hinges.

MICHEAL O'SIADHAIL

THE ENCHANTED HORSE

(for Maria at bedtime)

What can I promise this pyjamaed Miss? Nothing
and everything. A moment's falling stillness,
as above the duvet, hands cross in listening.
This horse is a gift only the promised can promise.

Between your ragdoll and the button-nosed bear
sleep wings and lapses. Images, fantasy,
trickery, foolishness, sudden flights of wonder
as we become the words we tell. Trust me.

A day's joys and bruises begin to heal
in delicious expectation. The prince outwits
a wicked sultan of Cashmere. All's well!
Ride the enchanted horse to Bengal's palace.

Those brows and lashes oval and succumb.
Such a powerful wizard! At his command
like wasps around a ripening plum
stars fly down to settle in his hand.

And the court gasped as the horse took off.
From every word Scheherazade's fate spun;
minute by minute teller and listener grow,
woven in the telling giver and getter are one.

A story within a story. So now Missy
you're that princess near the summer-house
hidden amid the lilac, the jasmine, the narcissi.
Magician, I bridle with dreams your ebony horse.

ELIZABETH JENNINGS (England)

A CHILD DESTROYED

I can do nothing but feel, I can imagine
The terror within the mind of that child who was carried
Away from a moment of play. Was it a happy regret?
What did she see in her mind's eye? The T.V. children's programme?
He held the stinking cloth against her mouth
And she must have smelt tobacco, dirt, male stenches.
She tried to scream. She kicked him and he gripped
Her legs together, pinioned arms behind her.
Again and again I turn to my own childhood
When fears were but imaginary ones.
My only pains concussion or pneumonia,
And they seem honours as I try to force
Myself into this child's little shoes
And dear white socks, and soft washed hair, and then
I bring her start in life to bear on me.
She knew of love in night-time kisses, hugs
And kind hands holding hers. Now this large weight,
The man's cruel body forcing her to lie
Under his. I hear her small frock torn,
I hope by then she was unconscious but
She may have felt the thrust and heave of sex,
Smelt the man's breath, and then he gripped her neck
And twisted it as if it were a bird's
Or else a rabbit's. So our world behaves,
We have grown lax and comfort-loving, watched
The act of sex on big screens in the dark,
Have eaten, drunk, too much. We are to blame
And this small, broken, violated child
Must be the scapegoat. I'm ashamed and hate
The helplessness I feel, my world's cruel work.

A major renewal of effort to protect the lives and the development of children, and to end the worst aspects of poverty, would be the greatest long-term investment which the human race could make in its future economic prosperity, political stability, and environmental integrity. The time to make that investment is now. One and a half billion children will be born in the decade of the 1990s and, towards the end of that decade, a historic turning point will be reached as the number of children being born into the world finally reaches its peak and begins to decline. It is UNICEF's most fundamental belief, as the world struggles to free itself from the old preoccupation with war, that there could be no more important *new preoccupation* than protecting the lives and the development of the largest generation of children ever to be entrusted to mankind.

RUTH FELDMAN (U.S.A.)

FOURTH STREET

I was Elaine the lily maid,
dead of my love
for Lancelot, my bier
raised on a blackpalled barge,
and oared upriver
by a faithful mute. I was
the Lady of Shalott,
pacing her tower murmuring:
"I am half sick of shadows".

The neighbours told my mother
I passed them without speaking.
I didn't dare insist
I hadn't seen them.

After her death, I found
my mother's verses buried
in a drawer. My throat
aches with the not telling.

FUN HOUSE

I tripped on an old tune tonight
and plunged to the bottom
of the Fun Pier's giant slide;
I could not climb back up
the years' steep walls...

    A family friend
    who'd borrowed me for the afternoon
    led me across solid-seeming floors
    where jets of air blew my skirt
    over my head, sat me on benches
    that caught my scalloped sash.

    That same summer
    an old man carried me halfway out
    into the Atlantic and ducked me.
    Another lied me onto a rollercoaster:
    when I got off, my knees shook so
    that I could hardly stand.

    My own father,
    taking a useless cure, (his malady
    lay too deep for water's purging)
    swore I could safely drink from one
    fountain at the Spa, laughed
    when I wrinkled up my face and spat out
    the evil-tasting stuff.

I never learn. My chin sticks out
a mile.

RUTH FELDMAN

THE CHILD WHO WAS NEVER YOUNG

went to the circus with her friend
and her friend's father.
They went to the sideshow first;
her heart felt trapped
when she saw the animals
pacing back and forth
back and forth
with barely room to turn.

The midgets loved her
because she didn't stare
or make unkind remarks. They asked her name
and tried to pronounce it
in their foreign way; Rút,
they kept saying, Rút,
and tried to take her small hand
in their smaller ones.
She didn't look at the monstrous Things
in bottles, was embarrassed for the Fat Lady.

Under the big tent,
the child who was never young
didn't know which of three rings to watch
and always watched the wrong ones.
Her head swam when the high-wire cyclist
inched his way through hostile air
and she clutched the seat
to keep from falling.

She was humiliated for the elephants,
forced to cavort in the pink
obscenity of tutus.
She remembered Jungle Tales
and a different kind of elephant dance.

The child who was never young
had never been to a museum
and gasped when the curtain went up
on the Living Statues.
She wished the people and horses,
whitened to marble,
would hold poses and breath forever.

She flinched
when thunder cracked its whip
and made the lions nervous.
She was glad to leave
when the trainer caught his whip
for a long moment
in the cage bars.

The child who was never young
huddled close to her friend
under the umbrella,
clutching her cotton candy.
When she reached home she found
she was holding a cardboard cone.

SEAMUS HEANEY

THE WISHING CHAIR

When you sat, far-eyed and cold, in the basalt throne
Of "the wishing-chair" at Giant's Causeway,
The small of your back made sense of the firmament.

Like a papoose at sap-time strapped to a maple-tree,
You gathered force out of the world-tree's hardness.
If you stretched your hand forth, things might turn to stone.

But you were only goose-fleshed skin and bone,
The rocks and wonder of the world were only
Lava crystallized, salts of the earth

The wishing chair gave savour to, its kelp
And ozone sharpening your outlook
Beyond the range of possibility.

CLARIBEL ALEGRÍA (Nicaragua)

MI PARAISO DE MALLORCA

Todas las noches
en mi paraíso de Mallorca
surgen nuevos fantasmas:
oscuras quejas enredadas
al canto de los ruiseñores
llantos de niño,
miradas de veinte años
ya marchitas
que me opacan el cielo.
Es verano
y el mar está tibio
y huele a algas
y hay deseo en las cuencas
de tus ojos
y otro oleaje verde
de otro mar
de mi infancia
me golpea en el pecho
un veintidós de febrero por la tarde,
al otro día de morir Sandino
y yo no sabía
quién era Sandino
hasta que mi padre
me explicó
mientras saltábamos sobre las olas
y yo nací.
Como Venus,
vi por la primera vez la luz
entre la espuma.
Antes era una hierba,
una expiega alocada
que flotaba en el viento,
un par de ojos incontaminados
y vacíos.
Salí del mar
— mi mano entre la mano de mi padre —
odiando al ministro yanqui
y a Somoza
y esa misma noche
hice un pacto solemne
con Sandino
que no he cumplido aún

y por eso me acosa
su fantasma
y llega hasta mí el hedor
a represión
y no sólo es Sandino,
hice también un pacto
con los niños pobres de mi tierra
que tampoco he cumplido.
Cada cinco minutos
muere de hambre
un niño
y hay crímenes
y ghettos
y más crímenes
¡que a título del orden
¡se cometen,
¡de la lay y del orden
·y aunque el mar esté tibio
y yo te ame
mi paraíso de Mallorca
es un cuarto cerrado
y todas las noches se puebla de fantasmas.

22

CLARIBEL ALEGRIA

MY PARADISE IN MALLORCA

Every night
in my paradise in Mallorca
new ghosts appear:
vague groans, mingling
with the song of the nightingales,
a child's weeping,
faces of twenty-year-olds
already shrivelled up
darkening my sky.
It is summer
and the sea is lukewarm
smelling of seaweed
and there is desire in the valleys
of your eyes
and another green surge
from another sea
of my childhood
strikes me on the breast
one 22nd february in the afternoon,
the day after Sandino died
and I did not know
who Sandino was
until my father
explained
while we were leaping in the waves
and I was born.
Like Venus
I saw light for the first time
among the spray.
Before that I was a blade of grass,
a crazy ear of corn
floating in the wind
a pair of eyes, innocent
and empty.
I came up out of the sea
— my hand in my father's hand —
hating the Yankee minister
hating Somoza
and that very night I made
a solemn pact
with Sandino
which I have not yet carried out

and so his ghost
pursues me
and the stench of repression
reaches me
and it's not only with Sandino
I also made a pact
with the poor children of my land
and that too is not yet carried out.
Every five minutes
a child
dies of hunger
and there are crimes
and ghettoes
and still more crimes
committed in the name
of order, in the name
of law and order, and
although the sea is lukewarm
and although I love you
my paradise in Mallorca
is a locked room
and every night it is peopled by ghosts.

translated from the Spanish, by J.F.Deane

23

EAMON GRENNAN

TWO CLIMBING

After the blackface sheep, almond coats daubed
to the blush of slaughtered innards,
all I saw going up was a small frog
speckled rust and raw olive, slick as a
lizard, with a lizard's fixed
unblinking eye. It splays and tumbles
to a safe shadow where heather roots
wind through limestone and bare themselves
in tea-brown bolts of bog water, while I
keep climbing behind Conor, who's twelve, my heart
starting to knock at thin air, effort. He loves
leading me on, and when I look up
to where he stands waiting for me — legs apart
and firmly planted on a rock spur, gazing
round him at the mountains and the sea, at the
thin ribboning road beige below us, at my figure
bent over the flat green hands of bracken —
I'm struck sharp as a heart pain
by the way this minute brims
with the whole story: such touched fullness
and, plain as day, the emptiness at last.

2.

Once down again, safe home, we both
look wondering up to the top of Tully Mountain
and the barely visible concrete plinth
that peaks it, on which he sat
exalted for a time and took, he said,
the whole of Ireland in with one big
swivelling glance, and took twelve snaps
to prove it: a windy shimmer of cloud, mountain,
water — a rack of amphibian spirits
drifting over our heads. I saw the way our elevation
simplified the lower world to rocky crops
and patches, neat green and brown
trapezoids of grass and bog, bright pewtered spheres
of pure reflection. We sat out of the wind
on two flat rocks, and passed
in silence to one another
another sweet dry biscuit and a naggin
whiskey bottle of water, pleased with ourselves
at some dumb male thing for which he finds
the word: *adventure*. Going down,
he lopes, leads, is deliberately solicitous,
pointing out loose rocks, a safer way,
the treacherous bright green surface
of a swampy passage. His knowing talk
enlarges airily our trek and conquest.

3.

Walking at last the field path
to the house, he is all straight spine and
limber stride in his muddied wellingtons,
while I note how stone silent
the plum-coloured broad back of the mountain is, keeping
the wind off our lives in this hollow. Before going in,
he sets on an outside windowsill
the horned sheep skull we rescued
from the bracken, weathered to a cracked adze
of jawbone ringed and bristling
with broken teeth. Bone-flanged, the great
eye sockets gape, and, like fine stitching,
the skull's one partition seams dead centre.
In less than a week from now
he'll have forgotten this bony trophy,
but not the journey we took together to find it —
that hammering brisk ascent, the luminous
view of everything, those buffeting winds, unruffled
interlude of quiet, then, in the end,
that sweet leading down. While I'll go on
watching the split skull — colour of
crushed almond or washed-out barley muslin-shine.

EAMON GRENNAN

DAUGHTER AND DYING FISH

Cast out on this stone pier, the dogfish are dying
in a simmering sunlit heap of torcs
and contortions, bristlemouths propped open
in a silent scream against the treacherous
element of air, a yawn of pure despair, the soft slap
of fantails sliding the slow length of one another
as spines stiffen, scales slickly shimmer, glaucous
sea-eyes pop with shock and resignation when
my cloudy shadow trawls across them.
Against this, I have to stake my daughter
who balances her twenty months of life
on twisted arm-thick hands of rope and is no more
than a moment perplexed when she bends
to touch a spine, those fading scales, and then goes back
to the song she was singing, turning her back on what
I can't take my eyes off: their cloudy eyes,
the slow weave of their single limbs, a slubbered
smack of oily skin on skin, the faint heaving motion
of the whole mass like one body beating away
from the face of the earth. How they would glide
barely brushing one another, bodies all curve and urgency
in their glimmering space and humming chambers: quick
and fit and unpredictable, a swift unravelling of desire
or a terror of sleepy teeth, a swirl of shadow spelling death
to the freckled small fry who flick under cover and
feel the pull and swell of passage as, in a pounding silence,
the big fish slide by, who now lie waiting in the raw
elusive air for what comes next, a hapless
heap of undulant muscle, a faint, fierce throbbing. Gently
the sea slaps at these stone foundations
laid to stand the winter storms
without shaking: smooth as skin the granite surfaces
gleam under the sun, with here and there a pinpoint
dazzle of mica in limestone. I move to catch up
with my daughter who heads unsteadily
for the end of the pier - a cheerful small voice, still singing.

26

MÍCHEÁL Ó RUAIRC

SCEIMHLE

gur thugas abhaile na boinn
i mála páipéar donn,
greim scrogaill agam air
is gur thugas dom mháthair iad
d'fhonn milseáin a cheannach dom.
"Agus cá bhfuairis iad?"
ar sise liom.
"Thíos ag Teampail Flainn
i measc na bhfothracha, a mham."
"Ó Iosa Críost is a Mhuire Mháthair
tóg thar nais iad láithreach
mar tá gach máchail coirp
agus intinne ó aimsir Chroim
bailithe agat sa mhála sin.
Ná dúirt mé leat arís is arís eile
gan bacaint leosan, a bhuachaill?
Comharthaí aicí de agus fulaingte iadsan
fágtha ina ndiaidh acu
ag cruiteacháin is cláirínigh.
Tóg thar nais iad
nó scriosfar sinn",
ag gearradh Comhartha na Croise
idir í féin agus iad.
D'imíos le m'ualach damanta,
mo charn fulaingte agus screadanna
anuas le fána an chnoic
go bhfuaireas réidh
lem mhála mífhortún,
gach bonn péine scaipthe
go masmasach i measc
na gcarraigeacha beannaithe
agus ansin ag filleadh abahile
agus lagachair orm
agus an faitíos go rabhas galraithe
agus an oíche sin sa leaba
Ó, an sceimhle
roimh dhul a chodladh
go mbeinn im chruiteachán,
im chaláiríneach
nó im ghealt chríochnaithe
roimh theacht
na maidine

CARRIER

All I can now remember
is bringing home the coins
one morning in a brown
paper bag, gripped tightly
by the neck and giving
them to mother
so as to buy sweets for me.
"And where did you find them?"
she demanded, angrily.
"Down near the 'Round',
among the ruins"
I answered, innocently.
"Oh Holy Mary, Mother of God
what will I do with you!
Take them back at once
for you have gathered together
in that brown paper-bag
every mental and physical
deformity under the sun.
Haven't I told you before
to have nothing to do
with those coins?
Don't you know
that those are tokens
of disease and suffering
left after them by hunchbacks,
cripples and lunatics
hoping for miraculous cures.
Take them back at once
or we'll all be visited
by the sickness and suffering
contained in that brown paper bag,"
making the sign of the cross
between herself and me.
So off with me again
with my contaminated collection
of pennies and shillings,
my cache of pain and disease
down the hillside
as if all the demons in hell
were hot on my heels,
and filled with revulsion
I remember scattering the coins
among the holy ruins
and returning home again
overcome with fear and the horror
that I would become infected
and that night in bed,
oh, the dread
before going to sleep
of becoming
a hunchback, a cripple
or a raving lunatic
before waking up
the following morning

"The Children of Lir", by JOHN BEHAN

DESMOND O'GRADY

CHILDREN

Despite that protection a mother
provides for her every child;
despite the fertile powers old women
believe of the blossoming Mayflower,
whitethorn, blackthorn; our children —
beggars of their tomorrows —
will have their day and way,
will all turn cuckoo
and, like the cuckoo,
their hour come round,
they'll jump their fellows,
dump the lot on the jungle,
spread their wings of ambition
and fly off about their
own business crying:
Where? Where?
Seeking! Seeking!
For every son who'll become a maker,
his brother, to go one better,
will turn destroyer.
Their sister, if she carry
her cup properly,
may find a man can box his corner
and save a little
a while longer.

Transcending its detailed provisions,
the *Convention on the Rights of the Child*
embodies a fundamental principle
which UNICEF believes should affect
the course of political, social and
economic progress in all nations over
the next decade and beyond. That
principle is that the lives and the
normal development of children should
have *first call* on society's concerns and
capacities and that children should be
able to depend upon that commitment
in good times and in bad, in normal
times and in times of emergency, in
times of peace and in times of war, in
times of prosperity and in times of
recession. If the trench of such a
principle could be dug across the
battlegrounds of political and economic
change in the decade ahead, then
civilization itself would have made a
significant advance. The essence of
civilization is the protection of the
vulnerable and of the future: children,
like the environment, are both the
vulnerable and the future. Failure to
protect the physical, mental and
emotional development of children is
the principal means by which
humanity's difficulties are compounded
and its problems perpetuated.

THEO DORGAN

TWIN

I am a voice in towering stillness
I am the absence of that voice
And the child's coat it trails behind closed doors.
I am the memory you will never have,
Incident at the centre of your life.

I am the echo launched both ways at once,
Backward into the blue sea and forward
Into the arms of living death.
I am that death whose cry ripped out the echo,
Mine was the third voice of your conception.

When you first pulsed into a clot of flesh
Beating outward to the rosepink light,
I was the living measure of your need.
When the blue mesh built out beneath your skin,
Humming with blood and sugars,
I was the chord that sang you into life.

When you began the long, bloody slide
Into the lights and airs of this crazed planet,
I was the absence you already felt.
I was the echo fading in your wake,
I was the strongest contraction and the push,
The cry beating against you like white light.

I am the voice you search for and forget,
I am its absence for good reason,
Better to hunt for than to find —
Look in your father's and your mother's grave —
You die if you find me, die if you do not search.

ROBERT GREACEN

ON THE LANDING

I was sure he crouched on the landing
That one night he would puff my candle out
That my legs would give way
That he would laugh darkly
That he would carry me off
In a sack on his back.
Night after night I dilly-dallied
Invented excuses, mooned,
Doodled on blotting paper
Upset bottles of ink
Begged for mugs of buttermilk.
At last, sentenced to bed,
I loitered on the stairs
Stared at the yellow flame
Both sword and shield.
Then, desperate, reckless,
I shut my eyes
Ran as if Old Nick himself
Trod on my heels.
Secure in my attic room
I prayed as I'd been taught
Yet could not forget
That creature on the landing.

LARS GUSTAFSSON (Sweden)

Ballad före regnet

Allt är i väntan. Kastanjerna. Fåglarnas röster.
Det stora molnet som darar upp. Telefonen som ringer,
med ett förändrat ljud, vännen som talar om regn,
att vi behöver regn, om åskan som skall komma,
om vad han ser genom fönstret: det stora molnet som drar upp.
Kaprifolens doft starkare nu och jag minns barndomen.
Det är närmare nu. Alla ljud uppförstorade och underbara:
stadshusklockorna som inte brukar nå hit,
trastarna, skyggt tillbakadragna under trädens kronor,
ett barn som leker på gatan.
De levande cellerna skiljer sig från det döda
genom att komplicera sig, för varje hot
svarar den levande organismen
med en ny komplikation: allt finare sinnesorgan.
Jag vet inte. Något måste ha hänt. Ett skred,
en sättning, alltsammans är närmare nu.
I det nät av hemliga trådar och säkringar
som förbinder mig med och skyddar mig från
barndomen, dagarna, förflutenheten,
går en magnetisk störning. Signaler går fram,
lika främmande som om de kom
fran ett annat liv. Som på landet
när åskan är nära, och telefonerna ringer,
blint. Man svarar och hör alla traktens röster.
Denna morgon sprang jag, genom den tunga, fuktiga
försommarluften som ville bli regn,
sprang lycklig under den djupa grönskan,
och plötsligt _mindes_ jag något.
Det var i egg ögonblick när jag passerade
en fridsam metare, morgontidig, försjuken,
och mycket riktigt fick han i det ögonblicket
helt överraskande napp, en mörk och rasande gädda.
Så fick vi båda något: Han minnet. Jag fisken.
Eller omvänt, det kvittar egentligen lika.
Båda sprattlade ett ögonblick levande,
detta minne, denna rasande fisk.

"A Tumble of Crows", oil and collage, by TONY O'MALLEY

LARS GUSTAFSSON

BALLAD BEFORE RAIN

All is in waiting. The chestnut trees. The voices of the birds.
The great cloud that gathers. The telephone that rings
with an altered sound, the friend who speaks of rain,
that we need rain, that if demanded will come,
of what he sees out the window: the great cloud that gathers.
The scent of honeysuckle stronger now, and I remember childhood.
Now it is closer. All sounds amplified and wondrous:
the belltower of the city hall that usually doesn't reach here,
the thrush resting shyly in the crowns of the trees,
a child who plays in the street.
The living cells separate from the dead
by compounding themselves, for every threat
the living organism counters
with a new structure: a continually finer membrane.
I don't know. Something must have happened. A landslide,
a sinking, all of it is closer now.
In the threaded and fused web of secrets
that connects me with and protects me from
childhood, the days, the past,
a magnetic impulse passes. The signals are transmitted
as strangely as if they were coming
from a different life. As out in the country
when thunder is near, and the telephone rings
blindly. One answers and hears all the voices of the countryside.
This morning I ran through the heavy damp
early summer air that wanted to become rain,
ran happily beneath the deep greenery,
and suddenly I *remembered* something.
At a moment when I was passing by, there was
a peaceable fisherman, up early, absorbed,
and, sure enough, in that moment he got
an altogether surprising bite, a dark and furious pike.
So both of us got something: He the memory. I the fish.
Or vice-versa, it really makes no difference.
Both flopping around a moment alive,
this memory, this raging fish.

(translated from the Swedish by Robert Hedin, U.S.A.)

ROLF JACOBSEN (Norway)

Måne før det blir mørkt

En såpboble flagrer bort og brister over parkenes
løvgrotter og f ontenenes skum.
Små barn ser den og vil fange den i sine
hender

Langt use i de hvise kveldene løftes det
en fakkel. Det er et signal til høsten:
Kjør inn, ditt spor er klart.

Senere ser vi oftest månen som en grå
skalle som venter på oss use bak kveidens
glassklokke. Den står ganske stille og
banker på den med sin knokkel for
høre om vi er levende eller døde.

ROLF JACOBSEN (Norway)

MOON BEFORE IT BECOMES DARK

A soapbubble floats off and bursts over the parks'
leafy grottos and fountain spray.
Small children see it and want to catch it
in their hands.

Far out in the white evenings a torch
is lifted. It's a sign to the fall:
Drive in, your path is clear.

Later we often see the moon as a gray
skull waiting for us behind the evening's
glass bell. It stands perfectly still
and knocks with its bony knuckle
to hear whether we are living or dead.

(translated from the Norwegian by Robert Hedin U.S.A.*)*

UFFE HARDER (Denmark)

TALE TIL EN SON

Dine sindrige konstruktioner
eksperimentelle og monumentale
skamler stole brædder og kasser
anvendt som klodser
som mærkelige meningsfulde
nye organismer.
Dit hastige løb gennem stuerne
som om du styrede
et ukendt befordringsmiddel
og vore ceremonielt indledte
samtaler i hvilke vi utvungent bevæger os
fra emne til emne
nu skal vi tale om heste
dine bifaldsytringer
efter nøje vurdering
og de mere uforbeholdne
over for visse af livets goder
hurra
først og fremmest
din venlighed
og din evne til at dele
f.eks. rosiner
som du henter ud af munden
til fælles nydelse.

SPEECH FOR A SON

Your clever constructions
experimental and monumental
stools chairs planks and boxes
used as toy bricks
into strange and meaningful
new organisms.
Your quick running through the rooms
as if you steered
an unknown vehicle
and our conversations ceremonially begun
in which we move without constraint
from one subject to another
so now let's speak of horses
your approving remarks
after a thorough examination
and the more spontaneous ones
before certain good things in life
hurrah
above all
your friendliness
and your capacity to share
raisins for example
which you fetch out of your mouth
to be enjoyed in common.

(translated from the Danish by Uffe Harder)

THOMAS KINSELLA

THE BOYHOOD OF CHRIST

When He was barely five
Jesus, the Son of God,
blessed twelve water puddles
He moulded out of clay.

He made a dozen birds
— the kind we call the sparrow —
He made them on the Sabbath,
perfect, out of clay.

A Jew criticized Him
— Jesus, the Son of God! —
and to His Father Joseph
took Him by the hand.

"Joseph, correct your son,
he has committed wrong.
He made clay shapes of birds
upon the Sabbath day."

Jesus clapped His palms,
His little voice was heard.
Before their eyes — a miracle —
the little birds flew off.

The sweet, beloved voice was heard
from the mouth of Jesus pure:
"So they will know who made you
off with you to your homes."

A man who was there told everyone
the wonderful affair
and overhead they all could hear
the singing of the birds.

(translated from the 7th century Irish)

THOMAS KINSELLA

A SPIRIT

I left the road where a stile entered the wood,
with branches in the way everywhere, pine trees
standing close in their own flour.

Face to face, on a patch of bark, with a mouse body
staring upside down, the flesh distinct
and small, the wings flat.

Designed to be half seen high in the last light
— leather angel falling everywhere,
snapping at the invisible.

DENNIS O'DRISCOLL

ISSUE

1.

How delicate you'd look
in the first flush of pregnancy,
the curled lip puffed to a bud.

What will happen to the love
which, swollen as a pitcher,
you might have borne

and poured like broken waters
on the cracked foundation stone
of a fontanelle?

I love through you the children
whom, cell by cell,
we didn't build up

and I share the loneliness you feel
as if they'd grown and left home
adding, one by one, to your abandonment.

2.

Let's put names on the children
we'll never have - Kate, say (after
my mother), Rose (after yours).

Two more mouths to feed and kiss,
two long-haired girls (your nose,
my eyes) to brush and bind with slides.

They would conspire against us sometimes
or, teenagers out late, we'd check
the bedside clock, listen for their steps...

As we speculate this way,
they are no longer figments
but our baby daughters come to life,

their transparent hands deploying tiny nails,
their heads like fragile, blue-veined breasts,
their safety pins unclasping into fetus shapes.

With few exceptions, what we are in fact seeing is the exact opposite of the principle that the growing minds and bodies of children should have first call on the protection of society. Yet somehow the chilling injustice of what is happening is escaping our attention, passing by our windows on the smooth flow of economic analysis, disguising itself in the respectable clothing of the financial vocabulary. We are intermittently told that we are muddling through, a repayment rescheduled here, a debt written down there, masking from our view the closed clinic, the empty desks at school, the unvaried diet, the anaemic mother, the child who never puts on weight.

On present trends, more than 100 million children will die from illness and malnutrition in the 1990s. These children will not be the victims of any sudden flood or famine. There will be no televeision cameras at their deaths, no public outrage, no demand for action. They are children who will die little noticed by the world. The causes of those deaths can be listed on the fingers of one hand. Almost all of those children will die of diseases which were once just as familiar in the industrialized nations. They will die in the sunken-eyed coma of dehydration, or in the gasping extremities of pneumonia, or in the iron grip of tetanus, or in the fever of measles, or on the rack of whooping cough. These five common illnesses, all relatively easy and inexpensive to prevent or treat, will account for two-thirds of all child deaths and over half of all child malnutrition in the decade which lies ahead.

JULIE O'CALLAGHAN

JASPER YAWNING

Jasper knows the score
so you can forget it — he is not impressed.
He doesn't care about current events
or the weather — he hangs around
in a woolen blanket
and a lime green snap-up-the-front number
with embroidered lamb.
He keeps out all brain pollution
with a really radical red and white striped
anti-hogwash baby bonnet,
with optional under-the-chin tie string.
Give yourself a break
and dispense with piggys going to market
and goochy-goochy-goos:
this guy hates to see an adult
making an idiot of himself.
His ear-flaps automatically
intercept all baby talk.
He's waiting for his face to grow bigger
because right now
when people take his photograph
or pat him on the back
to make him burp
or tickle him under his arm
or tell him how cute he is
the scope of his yawn is limited —
his eyes and nose keep getting in the way.
But hey, that's just technical —
you're either born a boredom detector
or you ain't, end of story.
I'll zip my lip —
his mouth is starting to quiver.

TOM MAC INTYRE

PROFESSION

The grandmother caught
the red gansy's flit
at the turn of the lane,

got there in time
to see that red melt
the next turn, let

out a roar, salted,
put down the boot,
did sums, found him

in The Hill Field,
easy as you like, with
a calf by the tail...

She knew then, she
always claimed after,
cut of the child,

calf nose in the air,
July day an oven.
Back to a sycamore,

she watched from the shade.

GERARD SMYTH

COMFORTER

She presses her breasts to streaming tears.
Once again she's a child's comforter

washing blood and dirt from scraped knees
or soothing a nervous imagination
awake at night in the silent house.

She is the story-teller, the water-carrier
who is never more serious than when she's looking
for a lost splinter in the palm of a hand

or turning the cool underside of a pillow
towards cheeks inflamed by the childhood fevers.

PADRAIG J. DALY

DUVET

Knowing my love of comfort, warmth and sleep,
Some friends gave me a great feathery eiderdown
To ease my Winters.

It will take me like Sinbad
Into lands of strange giants and peoples.

I will unfurl it to the wind
And sail like Brendan round half the world.

I will make a cloak of it like Bodach an Chóta Lachtna
And when I stretch my arms
Kingfishers, wrens and tiny birds of every colour
Will whoosh from under it.

I will make a tent of it,
Stretched on poles as Yahweh stretched the sky.

It will be my sunshade near warm tides,
My bivouac in lands of snow.

I will spread it on the ground like the Roman widow
And build my basilica on top.

I will put it down on swamps
And build a bridge.

I will line my hollow walls with it
And insulate my ceiling.

It will be my meadow of Summer flowers
In dark December,
My noisy cataract, my Comeragh lake.

May the Lord prosper those who gave it,
Fill their mouths with music,
Bathe their bodies in buttermilk.

May their sheep lamb twice each year,
Their hens lay double eggs,
Their cows flood Ballyclough with cream.

It will teach me to think kindly on human hearts;
And on the heart of God
Who covers us always with undeserved kindness.

CIARAN O'DRISCOLL

A RUMOUR OF SPIRIT

I'm researching a rumour of spirit
in a library of metal-plated shelves.
Fluorescent tubes of light are set to cool
in metal grids that cling to a blue ceiling.
The wall beside me is half-stripped of plaster,
an authentic work-in-progress whose essence
is to conceal and yet reveal the neat
fastidious handicraft of red brick.
Under its chalky surface what protects us
from the summer day's persistent heaviness,
the spirit's enemy inducing flesh
to seek a key, an entry point into
its old density and concentration
among disjunctive individuals
that to and fro in torrid heat outside,
a happy, brief togetherness of atoms,
is brick upon mortared building brick.
We live in the age of repetition
as Warhol's reproducible Marilyn
has proved, while the unique original
overdoses on the absence from itself.
In every library in the universe,
a calendar open at May and June
has a picture of ringed plovers on a beach,
the female sitting over speckled eggs.
There's a thistle in the foreground, and the shingle
is littered with scallop and mussel shells.

RICHARD MURPHY

CARE

Kidded in April above Glencolumbkille
On a treeless hill backing north, she throve
Sucking milk off heather and rock, until

I came with children to buy her. We drove
South, passing Drumcliff. Restless in the car,
Bleating, she gulped at plastic teats we'd shove

Copiously in her mouth. Soon she'd devour
Whatever we'd give. Prettily she poked
Her gypsy head with hornbuds through barbed wire

To nip off pea-tops, her fawn pelt streaked
With Black Forest shadow and Alpine snow.
I stalled her wildness in a pen that locked.

She grew tame and fat, fed on herbs I knew
Her body needed. We ransacked Kylemore
To bring her oakleaf, ivy and bark to chew.

I gutted goatbooks, learning how to cure
Fluke, pulpy kidney, black garget, louping ill:
All my attention bled to cope with her.

No commonage to roam unfenced, no hill
Where she could vanish under a dark cloud
To forage with a puck-led flock: but the dull

Grind of small children bucketing her food,
Yelling across a yard. Out in a forest
She would have known a bad leaf from a good.

Here, captive to our taste, she'd learnt to trust
The petting hand with crushed oats, or a new
Mash of concentrates, or sweet bits of waste.

So when a child mistook a sprig of yew
And mixed it with her fodder, she descried
No danger: we had tamed her instinct too.

Whiskey, white of egg, linseed oil, we tried
Forcing down antidotes. Nothing would do.
The children came to tell me when she died.

CHARLES TOMLINSON (England)

THE PICTURE OF J.T. IN A PROSPECT OF STONE

What should one
        wish a child
                and that, one's own
emerging
        from between
                the stone lips
of a sheep-stile
        that divides
                village graves
and village green?
                — Wish her
                        the constancy of stone.
— But stone
        is hard.
                — Say, rather
it resists
        the slow corrosives
                and the flight
of time
        and yet it takes
                the play, the fluency
from light.
        — How would you know
                the gift you'd give
was the gift
        she'd wish to have?
                — Gift is giving,
gift is meaning:
        first
                I'd give
then let her
        live with it
                to prove
its quality the better and
        thus learn
                to love
what (to begin with)
        she might spurn.
                — You'd
moralize a gift?
        — I'd have her
                understand
the gift I gave her.
        — And so she shall
                but let her play
her innocence away
        emerging
                as she does
between
        her doom (unknown),
                her unmown green.

44

"Children Returning from the Blessing of the Lilies, Dublin 16 June 1939", Lithograph by LOUIS LE BROCQUY

DENISE LEVERTOV (England and U.S.A.)

COMPLICITY

On the young tree's highest twig,
a dark leaf, dry, solitary, left over
from winter, among the small new buds.
But it turns its head!
                    It's a hummingbird,
tranquil, at rest, taking time off
from the hummingbird world of swift intensities —
yet no less attentive. Taking
a long and secret look at the day,
like a child whose hiding-place
has not been discovered, who hasn't even
been missed. No hue and cry.
                    I saw
a leaf: I shall not betray you.

KATHLEEN RAINE

"LITTLE CHILDREN HAVE KNOWN ALWAYS"

Little children have known always
What Plotinus taught the wise,
That the world we see, we are,
Soul's country beyond time and place
Her bright self-image in a glass,
Tree, leaf and flower,
Sun, moon, and farthest star.

JACQUES RANCOURT (France)

LA DISTRIBUTION DES CORPS

Avec tout le temps qu'il fait
chacun en a pour son argent
ou l'argent qu'il n'a pas

c'est un peu la même chose
mais c'est aussi l'inverse

ce n'est pas qu'une question d'argent
d'ailleurs

d'ailleurs
tout commence
à la distribution des corps

il y en a pour tout le monde
il n'y en a qu'un chacun
pour toute une vie

il y a bien de quoi fumer sa pipe
ce n'est pas la fumée qui s'en plaindra

il vaut mieux ne pas se plaindre
d'ailleurs

d'ailleurs
les plus à plaindre ne font qu'un bruit de fond

Avec tout le temps qu'il fait
et les absences qu'il a

le jeu des corps

pèse sur l'âme
et l'âme arrive trop tard pour porter plainte

c'est aussi une question d'argent
d'ailleurs

D'ailleurs
Avec tout l'argent qu'il fait
et le temps c'est encore de l'argent

les uns tirent le meilleur du pire
d'autres font des tabacs

il y en a qui n'ont rien à tirer
ils tirent la queue du diable

A la distribution des corps
tous les hommes sont égaux
à eux-mêmes

le reste n'est que du vent
qui se perd dans l'espace

le reste dépend du vent
qui opère dans l'espace

Car
avec tout le vent qu'il fait
sans parler de l'espace
mais parlons-en

Car
avec tout l'espace qu'il fait
et le emps c'est l'espace en plus

le vent souffle à discrétion
il souffle infiniment

Dieu sait pourquoi dans les planètes
personne n'a trové
enseigne où porter plainte

il y a du vent dans la voilure
il ya du sang dans l'embrasure

le choeur des corps ne fait qu'un bruit très sourd

49

THE DISTRIBUTION OF BODIES

With all the time that falls about us
everyone has some for his money
or the money he hasn't got

it's more or less the same thing
but it's also the other way around

it's not only a question of money
moreover

moreover
it all begins
with the distribution of bodies

there is some for everyone
there is only one to each person
for a whole lifetime

now there's a good reason for smoking one's pipe
it's not the smoke that will complain

it's better not to complain at all
moreover

moreover
those who complain most merely make scratching noises

With all the time that falls about us
and the blackouts that there are

the game of bodies
weighs heavily on the soul
and the soul comes too late to lodge a complaint

it's also a question of money
moreover

Moreover
With all the money that falls about us
and time of course is still money

some can make the best of a bad job
others can make a very great deal

there are some who have nothing to pull on
they pull the devil's tail

(translated from the French by J. F. Deane)

At the distribution of bodies
all men are equal
to one another

anything else is merely wind
that loses itself in space

anything else depends on the wind
that operates in space

For
with all the wind there is about us
without speaking of space
but let us speak of it

For
with all the space there is about us
and time is space besides

the wind comes blowing where it will
blowing infinitely about

God knows why among the planets
no one has ever found
somewhere to lodge complaints

there is wind up in the shroud
in the recess blood is to be found

the choir of bodies makes only a very dull sound

50

LESLIE ULLMAN (U.S.A.)

PRIVATE ACTS

My father promised,
as he shut my door, night
was the sun's eye
blinking. I promised

I wouldn't chew paper
again, or leave the damp wads
like amulets under the bed.
I shut my eyes. The guests

raised their drinks and told stories
downstairs, laughing in their
bracelets. Their rings of smoke.
Their strange breath bloomed

with attention. I opened my eyes
but the paisley sofa rose
anyway, a copper wave that filled
and kept filling my eye's black room.

I crept to the stairs where light
floated up, and sometimes
a string of words I wanted
to wear for the night...

He tucked me in again.
He promised me dark
as a pair of arms, rocking
water, a blanket my size...

The paper tasted salty,
the taste of my first lie.
Then I crept into the waves
of scented furs on the bed no one

made my parents sleep in —
no, I slept all night
in the bed where I
belonged, while turquoise threads

branched like bits of sky
through my mother's water-colored
gown, and the gray morning
leaked into all the windows at once.

It is the particular responsibility of government, in both industrialized and developing worlds, to set the parameters for a new deal for children in the 1990s. In the lessening of regional and ideological conflicts, in the beginning of progress towards disarmament, and in the birth of a new global awareness of environmental issues, it is possible that, as Soviet Foreign Minister Eduard Shevardnadze has put it: "A new political intellect is prevailing over the dark legacy of the past." If the twenty-first century is to be a better one for mankind than the

RICHARD KELL

AN AFRICAN BOY *(for Paul Lomongin, enquiringly)*

When Karamojan warriors
resisted government troops,
victims of the crossfire
fled from shattered homes
to the bleakness of the hills.

Children were missing later;
many had lost their lives.
But you, nine years of age,
"favourite subject maths,
hoping to be a teacher",
smiled into the lens.

Letters weren't allowed.
You sent a pencil drawing —
huts and a single tree;
I a Christmas card —
sheep in a winter sunset,
a note explaining snow.

Then the policy changed:
no sponsoring in future.
Although they'd use the cheques,
I couldn't help recalling
a film about a river
slowing to a marshy end
somewhere in the savannah.

But now I'd rather think
of water gliding deeply
towards a dazzling sea.
Dear Paul, I hope a friend
working in Karamoja
will help you dream that picture
and ask you what it means.

twentieth has been, then it is essential
that the principle of first call for
children become a part of that new
political intellect. It is within our power
to end child deaths, child abuse, child
illness, and child malnutrition on the
scale which defaces our civilization
today. And it is within our power to
ensure that every child has a school to
go to, a health worker to refer to, and a
diet which allows normal mental and
physical growth.

THOMAS LYNCH (U.S.A.)

GRIMALKIN

One of these days she will lie there and be dead.
I'll take her out back in a garbage bag
and bury her among my sons' canaries,
the ill-fated turtles, a pair of angelfish:
the tragic and mannerly household pests
that had the better sense to take their leaves
before their welcomes or my patience had worn thin.
For twelve long years I've suffered this damned cat
while Mike, my darling middle-son, himself
twelve years this coming May, has grown into
the tender if quick-tempered manchild
his breeding blessed and cursed him to become.
And only his affection keeps this cat alive
though more than once I've threatened violence —
the brick and burlap in the river recompense
for mounds of furballs littering the house,
choking the vacuum cleaner, or what's worse:
shit in the closets, piss in the planters, mice
that winter indoors safely as she sleeps
curled about a table-leg, vigilant
as any knick-knack in a partial coma.
But Mike, of course, is blind to all of it —
the grey angora breed of arrogance,
the sluttish roar, the way she disappears for days
sex-desperate once or twice a year,
urgently ripping her way out the screen door
to have her way with anything that moves
while Mike sits up with tuna fish and worry,
crying into the darkness "here kitty kitty",
mindless of her whorish treacheries
and or of her crimes against upholsteries —
the sofas, love seats, wingbacks, easychairs
she's puked and mauled into dilapidation.
I have this reoccurring dream of driving her
deep into the desert east of town
and dumping her out there with a few days feed
and water. In the dream, she's always found
by kindly tribespeople who eat her kind
on certain holy days as a form of penance.
God knows, I don't know what he sees in her.
Sometimes he holds her like a child in his arms
rubbing her underside until she sounds
like one of those battery powered vibrators
folks claim to use for the ache in their shoulders.
And under Mike's protection she will fix her
indolent green-eyed gaze on me as if
to say: Whaddya gonna do about it, Slick,
the child loves me and you love the child.
Truth told, I really ought to have her fixed
in the old way with an air-tight alibi,
a bag of ready-mix and no eyewitnesses.
But one of these days she will lie there and be dead.

And choking back loud hallelujahs, I'll pretend
a brief bereavement for my Michael's sake,
letting him think as he has often said
"deep down inside you really love her don't you Dad."
I'll even hold some cheerful obsequies
careful to observe God's never-failing care
for even these, the least of His creatures,
making some mention of a cat-heaven where
cat-ashes to ashes, cat-dust to dust
and the Lord gives and the Lord has taken away.
Thus claiming my innocence to the bitter end,
I'll turn Mike homeward from that wicked little grave
and if he asks, we'll get another one because
all boys need practice in the arts of love
and all boys' aging fathers in the arts of rage.

EILÉAN NÍ CHUILLEANÁIN

ALL FOR YOU

Once inside the strange stable yard, we dismount.
The donkey walks on, straight in at a wide door
And sticks his head in a manger.

The great staircase of the hall slouches back,
Sprawling between warm wings. It is for you.
As the steps wind and warp
Among the vaults, their thick ribs part; the doors
Of guardroom, chapel, storeroom
Swing wide and the breath of ovens
Flows out, the rage of brushwood,
Roots torn out and butchered.

It is for you, the dry fragrance of teachests
The tins shining in ranks, the ten-pound jars
Rich with shrivelled fruit, Where better to lie down
And sleep, along the labelled shelves,
With the key still in your pocket?

MACDARA WOODS

SUNFLOWERS

There was a moment I could have caught there
this afternoon on my steps
loose in the sunlight
seen fit to die here
looking down the hazy road toward Tavernelle
and the insects fluttering their day away
above my dusty sunflowers

There was a moment there I almost caught
when I recognised my father in myself
not the young man in photographs
foot on chair in revolutionary stance
but as I see him now
looking at me from the mirror
as I joke with my son about the motorcycle gobdaws
in the fields nearby
churning the red earth up

As I think we might have joked
reporting on the walkie-talkie
about the number of frogs in the irrigation ditch
since the coming of the water-snake
and gone for walks on the hill above the house
or dived for coins in the public pool
travelling together through the language
hand in hand
had we made it to Le Cigne
as we made it to the Shelly Banks

Age and drink dimmed that for us
still there was a moment there
I almost had us in a frame together
cycling through sunflowers down the Liffey Quays
that time you from the crowd
played stand-in for a missing goalie
in the Phoenix Park
forty years ago —
or dying for Ireland on the stage in Dublin
or checking your football pools in Sandymount
hopefully
on Sundays before the pubs opened
or hunting amethysts above Keem Bay for therapy

I remember this
middle-aged on these Italian steps
and understand the down-turn of your mouth
under siege and quizzical
echoed in my own
wondering how in the end we got here

Niall plays in the sunny yard below
I bequeath him summer and these sunflowers

MACDARA WOODS

LES CÔTES DU TENNESSEE

The colours you will walk in little son
these countries that are yours were mine
were magical and strange such contradictions
the space bat angel spread its wings
and came down burning from the sun —
are magical and strange and dangerous
and oh the world is full of crooks and heroes
beware the cargo when your ship comes in
the autumn serpent in the stubble field
those hungry spiders in our dusty rooms
have registered and taken note
and hold our image in their thousand eyes

Forty one years later the tune still plays
through this April afternoon my birthday
in the skies above the Lost River Ranch
Highway 76 and the Mississippi delta
Les Côtes du Tennessee and *Beausoleil*
the space bat dragon loops and sings
make me an angel that flies from Montgomery
make me a poster of an old rodeo
just give me one thing that I can hold on to
and the world is full of crooks and heroes —
I have been listening since East Liberty
since West Palm Beach and since the dawn

Vrai Citoyen du Monde of all the dawns
alone or shared in empty rooms
or standing by a ship's rail watching
this self-same Mississippi sun come up
down East of Wexford and the Tuskar Rock
in flight from time and circumstance — at
thirty thousand feet above pretence we start
to drop for Arkansas and South Missouri
new rooms new names new answers friends
as the space bat angel dragon sings
in a world made right for crooks and heroes
that if defeated we fly down in flames

MATTHEW SWEENEY

ECLIPSE

We got up to watch
the moon's eclipse
though no-one knew.

We set our clock,
then buried it
in Nathan's pillow.

We all got dressed,
opened the window
and climbed out

onto the roof,
the flat roof
of the new kitchen.

Look, said Sid.
There's a bite
out of the moon!

So there was.
A bite!, said Nathan.
Some dog!, I said.

Bite or not,
it slowly grew
bigger — night's

takeover, I thought,
and watching it
it seemed forever —

no more moon.
Moon dissolved
by space-acid,

earth next . . .
I shook my head.
Nightdreaming!

Sid was snoring.
Nathan woke him,
glanced behind.

I stared up
at the bright silver
the moon was.

Then it was gone.
All dark —
then it was back,

or another sliver,
the other side
of the moon.

We watched it grow,
or the shadow
pass across it

and as it looked
on course
for roundness

we climbed inside
and fell asleep
in minutes.

We were still asleep
at breakfast.
Didn't tell why.

JOHN F. DEANE

MIRRORS

The boy, standing.
His back to the bay window;
darkness behind, the folds of heavy curtains
not quite meeting; position, centre stage.

A hall-stand, with flowers, marigolds perhaps,
his right hand leaning on it, posed, his left
fingering the beads with their statement:
here is a strong and a perfect Christian.

He is gazing out at me with frank eyes,
that contained stance, those cauliflower ears.
I remember, but cannot recognize him.
I remember a bedroom, window sashes,

winds splashing through the pines outside,
dancehall music on the night air,
drums pounding and the vroom kavroom of a bass;
I lay unsleeping, waiting for voices,

laughter, and the slamming of car doors;
the wardrobe mirror had a silver sheen;
I rose and stood before its narrow door,
and someone older, cynical, unsure, gazed out at me.

Tragic and moving as pictures of starving children may be, the time has come to ask why the world reacts with outrage and demands action when a quarter of a million children are threatened by famine but remains unperturbed by the annual deaths of some 5 million young children from illnesses as simple and cheaply prevented as measles and dehydration. Amid so many other pressing concerns, it is difficult to find time on the world's agenda for problems which, it may be argued, have always been with us and cannot therefore be regarded as exceptional or urgent. But for the children who will unnecessarily fall to malnutrition, disease, disability, and an early death in the decade ahead, and for the families of those children, such an argument will carry very little weight. From the broader perspective of our common future, ensuring the healthy physical and mental development of children is the most important investment that can be made in the healthy social and economic development of our societies. Doing what can now be done to achieve that goal is therefore an issue worthy of its place on the agenda of the world's political leaders, the world's press, and the world's public, as we enter the last decade of the twentieth century.

PAT BORAN

CHILDREN

Children in ill-fitting uniforms
drive adults to school, and children
argue the cost of tobacco
in the Newsagent's nearby.

You must have noticed them.

And in the mornings they rise to slaughter pigs,
cook breakfast, solve crosswords at the office...
Or they send tiny adults into minefields,
barefoot, with pictures
of Khomeini around their necks,
their old toes searching the sand
for death.

And children queue for Bingo
on Ormond Quay, on Mary Street,
and douse their leaking take-aways with vinegar.

And children talk and smoke incessantly
in Eastern Health Board waiting rooms,
always moving one seat to the right,
someone's parents squabbling over trinkets
on the worn linoleum.

And it is always children
who will swear for their tobacco — children
with beards and varicose veins —
and children, dressed as policemen,
who pull their first corpses from the river.

And who is it who makes love in the dark
or in the light, who haunts
and who does all our dying for us,
if not children?

We leave their fingerprints
on everything we touch.

THE EXPANDING JUKEBOX

Today as we pass at dusk
through Castlecomer, the road
is a pilgrimage of shadows —
third-world children, dead
in such numbers their homelands
can not contain the ghosts.

Like us,
moths to a lamp, they are drawn
towards the promise of song.

PAT O'BRIEN

CHILDREN'S GAME, GUATAJIAGUA, EL SALVADOR

Heat has kilned the red earth
to the rough texture of pottery;
the rain season glazed on the surface
footprints of child and man, the lottery

of war, soldier and guerilla in turn
imprinting their design. Whose slogan
was last half-erased? What flag burns
over the civic building? When children

begin to play such questions cease.
In their faces battles and conquests
long ago have made a treaty of peace,
Spain and Pipil Indian at rest

in the delicate structures of bone.
They make a small circle in the ground.
Then three strides out a larger one.
Dead centre they place small coins.

There are three of them, each with a spinning-
top, hand-carved in hard wood
from forests which heard first the new tongue
and first knew the iron name of the iron God.

All is circular, coins and tops, the games
bounds. And overhead the sun keeps
vigilant eye on lands which once flamed
to its glory. Sun sweat and weeping

moon were gold and silver filigree —
not to be sold or bartered
but to be the labour and love of beauty.
The coins are the history of what happened.

The top is spun, orbitting planet, star-
fall, quick, sure. A dime flies outward
for the Aztec warrior. Childs laughter,
and the piazza is innocent of war.

We gather to marvel at the skill,
a cupped palm enfolds the still
spinning top and the game continues
until the last coin is spun from the circle.

Sun and fun are suddenly eclipsed,
an ill wind blows and a giant insect
shadow prowls. In the shattered sky
the spinning top of helicopters are cyclops eyes

with children in their deadly aim and sight.

EAGLE STAR

One Vision, One Star.

Michael Brennan, Managing Director, Eagle Star.

Eagle Star is very pleased to act as Sponsor to the publication of this book for UNICEF.

We think it is especially appropriate that Eagle Star should support the fundamental principle of UNICEF that "the lives and normal development of children should have first call on society's concerns and capacities and that children should be able to depend upon that commitment in good times and bad, in normal times and in times of emergency, in times of peace and in times of war, in times of prosperity and in times of recession".

In Eagle Star we see a shared purpose through our business in Ireland as a Life Insurance Company providing protection for families and children in times of need such as disability, or premature death of a parent.

We hope that this book will in some way help to progress towards some improvement in the 'State of the World's Children' into the 1990's and beyond.

Sincerely,

Michael Brennan